# Apple

MW00943144

# Operator's Manual

The Complete How-to-Guide for seniors and beginners to master the smartwatch in no time.

By

**Van McMahon**

## Table of Content

## Introduction

Apple introduced the Apple Watch Series 9 device in September 2023. In the dynamic realm of wearable technology, few devices have captivated the imagination and transformed daily life like the Apple Watch Series 9. A fusion of cutting-edge engineering and elegant design, this latest iteration represents the pinnacle of innovation in the smartwatch arena.

The Apple Watch Series 9 stands as a testament to Apple's unwavering commitment to pushing the boundaries of what wearable technology can achieve. With its sleek contours, vibrant Retina display, and an arsenal of features designed to enhance every facet of life, it is more than a timepiece—it is a companion, a health monitor, a communication hub, and a fitness coach, all seamlessly integrated into one wrist-worn marvel.

At a glance, the Apple Watch Series 9 exudes sophistication and craftsmanship. However, beneath its sleek exterior lies a wealth of capabilities waiting to be harnessed. This guide endeavors to demystify every facet of the Series 9 experience, from the initial setup to the mastery of its most advanced features. Whether you are a first-time wearer or a seasoned Apple Watch aficionado, this eBook is poised to be your trusted companion in navigating the intricacies of this extraordinary device.

The Series 9 introduces a panoply of enhancements, each tailored to elevate user experience to new heights. From an extended battery life that ensures uninterrupted usage throughout the day to advanced health monitoring features that empower users to take charge of their well-being, this eBook leaves no stone unturned in providing comprehensive insights into the Series 9's capabilities.

The eBook guides readers through the process of personalizing their Apple Watch, from selecting and customizing watch faces to organizing apps and notifications. It sheds light on the intricacies of health and fitness tracking, allowing users to make the most of the Series 9's robust suite of wellness tools. With detailed instructions on setting up and utilizing features like Fall Detection, ECG, and the Noise app, this guide ensures that users can confidently leverage these life-saving and health-enhancing functionalities.

The Apple Watch Series 9 is not an isolated entity; it is a seamless extension of the broader Apple ecosystem. This eBook elucidates how the Series 9 harmoniously interacts with iPhones, Macs, and other Apple devices, allowing users to effortlessly transition between them and enjoy a cohesive digital experience.

As we embark on this exploration of the "Apple Watch Series 9 Guide," it is with the understanding that this eBook is more than a manual; it is a passport to a world of limitless possibilities. It empowers users to unlock the full potential of their Series 9, transforming it from a mere accessory into an indispensable companion. Whether you're striving for optimal health, enhanced productivity, or seamless connectivity, the Apple Watch Series 9, paired with this guide, promises to be a catalyst for a more empowered and connected lifestyle. Together, let us delve into this digital odyssey, where the horizons are boundless, and the potential, boundless.

It has been nearly ten years since the first launch of the Apple Watch. Judging by its exterior, you might find it hard to discern the specific model of an Apple Watch, as there has been minimal change in its appearance over the years. Throughout its evolution, the enhanced internal components have transformed the Apple Watch. It has evolved from a somewhat luxurious accessory closely linked to your iPhone, into a truly indispensable standalone device. Before opening your Apple Watch, let's look at how the previous models have evolved over the years.

A Timeline of Apple Watch Evolution

**2014** — The Apple Watch was first announced by Apple's CEO, Tim Cook, on September 9, 2014. It was officially released on April 24, 2015. Initially, it was compatible only with iPhones.

**2016** — In September 2016, Apple introduced the Apple Watch Series 1 and Series 2. Series 1 featured the same internal components as the original Apple Watch but with an updated processor. Series 2 included GPS, a brighter display, and was water-resistant up to 50 meters.

**2017** — Released in September 2017, the Apple Watch Series 3 featured a dual-core processor and optional cellular connectivity. It allowed users to make calls, send messages, and stream music without needing to be tethered to an iPhone.

**2018** — The Apple Watch Series 4, introduced in September 2018, featured a significant redesign with a larger display and rounded edges. It also introduced health features like the ECG (electrocardiogram) and fall detection.

**2019** — Released in September 2019, the Apple Watch Series 5 introduced an always-on display, allowing users to see the time and complications at all times.

**2020** — In September 2020, Apple released the Apple Watch SE, a more budget-friendly option with many features similar to the Series 6, but lacking a few of the advanced health sensors. Released alongside the SE in September 2020, the Series 6 introduced a new blood oxygen sensor, faster charging, and an even brighter always-on display.

**2021** — Announced in September 2021, the Apple Watch Series 7 features a refined design with a larger, more rounded screen and improved durability.

Throughout the years, Apple has released several versions of its watch operating system, **watchOS**, introducing new features and improvements in **health monitoring, fitness tracking, and app capabilities**. Over time, Apple has increasingly emphasized the health and fitness capabilities of the Apple Watch, introducing features like heart rate monitoring, activity tracking, sleep tracking, and more. The Apple Watch has a vast ecosystem of third-party apps available through the App Store, ranging from fitness apps to productivity tools and more. Apple continues to invest in the development of the Apple Watch, with a strong emphasis on health-related features and capabilities.

What's New in Apple Watch Series 9?

The Series 9 comes in a slightly more compact packaging, crafted entirely from fiber materials. Even with the new packaging, you'll still find the Series 9 delivers the same premium unboxing experience that Apple products are renowned for. When you unbox your Series 9, you'll discover two boxes inside the white packaging: one for the smartwatch case itself and another for the strap of your choice.

You'll be pleased to know that with the Series 9, the wireless charger now boasts a braided cable for added durability. It's a very nice upgrade. As mentioned in the previous section, there have been no design changes between the Series 9 and last year's Series 8; they are essentially identical to each other. You still have the choice between 41mm and 45mm sizes. The casings retain their rounded edges, sapphire crystal backing, slim-bordered display, and Digital Crown with haptic feedback. Away from the similar design, here are the latest features on Apple's S9 Watch:

## S9 Double Tap

All you have to do to use the Series 9 is double-tap your index as well as thumb fingers. By simply double-tapping two fingers on the wrist of the Watch, S9 owners will easily respond to and finish calls, delay alarms, stop timers, play & pause songs, and much more in an inventive step towards availability. This is made feasible by an algorithm that recognizes distinct variations in hand motion when users touch their index and thumb simultaneously twice in a brief amount of time. The system integrates data from the gyroscope, accelerometer, and optical heart sensor. Wearers may double-tap the Apple's S9 to open the smart stack then double-tap it again to navigate among the widgets while it is on the home screen.

## The S9 SiP (Silicon Processor)

Despite the S9's huge, edge-to-edge screen, its internal components make it a more useful daily companion. Apple's S9 SiP, the novel Apple Silicon processor seen in the Apple Watch Series 9, will also be used in the Ultra 2 watch. With 5.6 billion transistors and a 30% quicker GPU, the revamped Apple Watch engine produces crisper animations and features. Currently, even when your smartphone is in a different room, the

Apple Watch S9 can locate it for you thanks to a second-generation hyper wideband processor. New HomePod connections are also included, enabling you to control neighboring HomePods as you get closer. With a 25% increase in dictation accuracy, the Series 9 exhibits superior voice processing capabilities.

## Detailed Siri Prompts

Improved Siri commands may now be handled on the S9 Watch without depending on cloud or mobile access thanks to the S9 SiP's 4-core cognitive engine. This allows the voice assistant to respond more quickly and, ideally, accurately. Customers will also benefit from a new Siri integration that makes it simpler to get health data via Siri and the Health app. Users of the Apple Series 9 watch may instruct Siri to register an exercise or ask it questions like "How many minutes did I rest last night?" Currently accessible in Mandarin and English, other languages will be added later.

## Additional Barbie-Themed Case

The brand-new pink aluminum casing for the Apple S9 watch is now for sale. This is a straightforward adjustment that many have anticipated and asked for. The starlight, pink, midnight, silver, or product (red) metal Apple Watch Series 9 will be available to customers. Additionally, a gold and graphite variant made of stainless steel will be offered.

Setting Up Your Apple Watch Series 9

The seamless integration between Apple's smartwatch and your iPhone allows for a smooth experience, enabling you to accomplish a multitude of tasks. However, before diving into its functionality, it's essential to ensure a proper setup. Here's a comprehensive guide to help you get started and make the most of your new wearable device.

**Power On and Pair**

Press and hold the side button until the Apple logo appears. Next, follow the on-screen instructions to select your language and region. Hold your iPhone near the watch to initiate the pairing process. A prompt will appear on your iPhone. Follow the instructions to complete the pairing.

## Set Up Basic Information

Select whether you'll be wearing the watch on your left or right wrist. Enter your Apple ID and password when prompted. Choose whether to enable features like Location Services, Siri, and Find My.

## Customize Watch Face and Complications

Swipe left or right to browse available watch faces. Tap on a face to select it. Customize the face by pressing firmly on the screen and selecting "Customize." Add complications (small widgets displaying information) by tapping areas of the watch face and selecting a relevant complication.

## Install Apps

Open the App Store on your Apple Watch. Browse or search for apps you'd like to install. Tap "Get" next to an app to install it.

## Configure Notifications

Open the Apple Watch app on your iPhone. Tap "Notifications" to customize which apps send notifications to your watch.

## Add Music and Podcasts

Open the Music app on your iPhone. Select songs or playlists to sync with your watch. For podcasts, use the Podcasts app to select episodes for offline listening.

## Customize Watch Settings

Open the Settings app on your Apple Watch. Adjust settings like Display & Brightness, Sounds & Haptics, and more. Discover and use features like the ECG app, Fall Detection, and Emergency SOS. Experiment with the Always-On Display, if applicable.

The Apple Watch Series 9 is a testament
to the pinnacle of design and
engineering. Let's delve into the
intricacies of its hardware, focusing on
design, display, and the impressive array
of sensors that power this cutting-edge
wearable.

The S9 Watch boasts **a sleek,
minimalist design** that seamlessly
blends form and function. Its casing,
available in 41mm and 45mm sizes,
maintains the signature rounded edges,
imparting a timeless aesthetic. The
refined craftsmanship is evident in every
detail, emphasizing Apple's commitment
to both style and durability.

The Series features a vibrant, high-resolution display that captivates the eye with its vivid colors and sharp clarity. The slim-bordered design maximizes screen real estate, ensuring an immersive experience whether you're checking notifications or navigating apps. This display is engineered to deliver visual brilliance, setting a new standard for smartwatch technology.

Using Apple's S9 watch, you will discover an impressive array of sensors, elevating its functionality to new heights. These sensors include:

1. **Heart Rate Sensor**: Continuously monitors your heart rate, providing valuable insights into your cardiovascular health and

enabling features like heart rate
notifications and ECG readings.

2. **Accelerometer and Gyroscope**:
   These precision sensors track
   your movements in three
   dimensions, facilitating accurate
   fitness tracking, fall detection, and
   other motion-related features.

3. **Ambient Light Sensor**:
   Automatically adjusts screen
   brightness based on ambient
   lighting conditions, optimizing
   visibility and conserving battery
   life.

4. **Electrocardiogram (ECG)
   Sensor**: Empowers you to take an
   ECG right from your wrist,
   providing critical data for
   assessing your heart's electrical
   activity.

5. **Blood Oxygen Sensor**: Offers insights into your blood oxygen levels, providing crucial information about your respiratory health.

6. **Built-in GPS**: Allows precise tracking of your outdoor activities, providing detailed maps and statistics for your workouts.

7. **Compass and Altimeter**: These sensors enhance navigation and tracking capabilities, particularly useful for outdoor enthusiasts.

8. **Always-On Altimeter**: Ensures real-time elevation information, perfect for hikers, climbers, and anyone interested in tracking changes in altitude.

The integration of these cutting-edge sensors not only expands the capabilities of the Series but also enhances its ability to support your health and fitness goals. In summary, the Apple Watch Series 9 redefines wearable technology through its impeccable design, stunning display, and a comprehensive suite of sensors. This remarkable fusion of aesthetics and functionality sets a new standard for smartwatches, delivering an unparalleled user experience.

watchOS 8: The Operating System Unleashed

The release of watchOS 8 marks a significant milestone in the evolution of Apple's wearable technology. Packed with a host of innovative features and enhancements, it takes the Apple Watch experience to an entirely new level. Let's explore the key highlights of this groundbreaking operating system.

## 1. **Redesigned Home Screen**:

watchOS 8 introduces a more intuitive Home Screen, allowing for quicker access to your favorite apps. The new grid view and list view options offer a more organized and personalized experience.

## 2. **Mindfulness and Health Features**:

A major focus of watchOS 8 is mental health and mindfulness. The "Reflect" app helps users practice mindfulness through short, guided sessions. Additionally, new breathing exercises and mindful notifications promote a sense of calm and well-being.

## 3. **Sleep-Tracking Enhancements**:

Building on the sleep-tracking feature introduced in the previous version, watchOS 8 now offers more detailed sleep analysis, including respiratory rate tracking. This provides users with valuable insights into their sleep quality and habits.

4. **Fitness+ Integration**:

The integration with Apple Fitness+ is seamless, with on-screen metrics during workouts and new workout types like Pilates and Tai Chi. This integration enhances the fitness experience and provides users with more options for staying active and healthy.

5. **Enhanced Messaging and Communication**:

watchOS 8 introduces new ways to connect with loved ones. The ability to send photos and GIFs directly from the Messages app, along with updates to the Scribble feature, makes communication more expressive and engaging.

## 6. **Focus Mode**:

This feature, shared with iOS 15, allows users to customize their notifications and app alerts based on their current activity or state of mind. It helps maintain focus and reduce distractions during specific tasks or moments.

## 7. **Improved Weather App**:

The Weather app receives a significant overhaul, providing users with more comprehensive and dynamic weather information. Interactive elements and full-screen maps offer a richer experience for keeping track of weather conditions.

## 8. **New Accessibility Features**:

watchOS 8 introduces powerful accessibility features, including AssistiveTouch and the ability to control Apple Watch with hand gestures. These advancements ensure that the device is more inclusive and accessible to a wider range of users.

## 9. **Always-On Display Enhancements**:

The Always-On Display is now even more functional, showing more information at a glance, including app-specific details. This feature provides a more convenient and customizable experience.

Adding Complications to Your Apple Watch Face

In Apple Watch Series 9, complications are small, customizable elements on the watch face that provide quick access to information or app shortcuts. They enhance the watch face's functionality by displaying real-time data or offering shortcuts to frequently used apps.

**Common Complication Options on Apple Watch**:

| Complicati on Type | Description |
|---|---|
| Date | Displays the current date. |
| Weather | Shows real-time weather conditions. |

| | |
|---|---|
| Activity Rings | Provides a visual representation of your daily activity progress. |
| Calendar | Displays upcoming events from your calendar. |
| World Clock | Shows the time in a different city or time zone. |
| Battery | Indicates the remaining battery percentage of your Apple Watch. |
| Heart Rate | Displays your current heart rate. |
| Noise Level | Monitor the ambient noise level in your environment. |

| | |
|---|---|
| Music | Offers quick access to playback controls for the Music app. |
| Timer | Allows you to set a timer for a specific duration. |
| Stopwatch | Functions as a stopwatch for timing activities. |
| Stocks | Provides real-time stock market information. |
| Sunrise/Sun set | Indicates the times for sunrise and sunset in your location. |
| Altimeter | Shows your current elevation. |

| Compass | Displays your current heading and cardinal direction. |
|---|---|
| Breathe | Offers guided breathing exercises for mindfulness. |
| Shortcuts | Provides quick access to user-defined shortcuts. |
| Reminders | Shows upcoming tasks and to-do items. |

Changing and Tweaking Apple Watch Faces:

- Firmly press the watch face to enter edit mode.
- Swipe left or right to select a watch face.

- Use the Digital Crown to scroll through available watch faces.

- Tap "Customize" to edit the selected watch face.

- Navigate through the customization options and use the Digital Crown or your finger to make adjustments.

- Tap the complication you want to change and use the Digital Crown to select a new one from the list of available complications.

Swipe left or right to see other watch faces.

Simple

Add features to your watch face.

Using the Apple Watch App on iPhone:

- Open the Apple Watch app on your iPhone.

- Tap "Face Gallery" to view and select watch faces.

- Customize the selected face to your preference.

- Tap "Add" to include complications, and drag them to

the desired position on the watch face.

- Remember to save your changes once you're satisfied with the customization.

The Digital Crown on Apple Watch Series 9

The Digital Crown is a key physical feature of the Apple Watch Series. It's a small, round button on the side of the watch that can be rotated and pressed. The Digital Crown serves multiple functions, acting as a versatile navigation tool and a customizable control.

Turning on the Digital Crown is not a separate step as it's an inherent part of the Apple Watch's design. It's always available for use. To interact with it, simply locate the small, round button on

the side of your Apple Watch and turn it
gently.

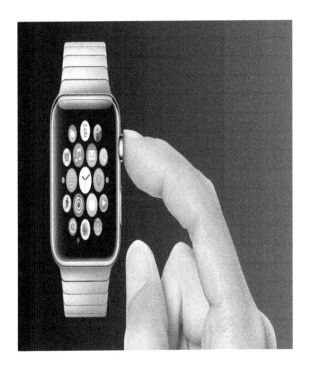

**10 Ways to Use the Digital Crown
Feature**

1. **Scrolling**: Gently turn the Digital
   Crown to scroll through lists,

messages, emails, and other content on the screen.

2. **Zoom In and Out**: In apps like Photos or Maps, turning the Digital Crown can zoom in or out for a closer look.

3. **Home Screen Access**: Press the Digital Crown once to return to the home screen from any app or function.

4. **Siri Activation**: Press and hold the Digital Crown to activate Siri. You can then speak your command or question.

5. **App Dock Access**: Press the Digital Crown twice to access the app dock, allowing you to quickly switch between frequently used apps.

6. **Notification Center**: When on the watch face, a gentle twist of the Digital Crown downwards will reveal the Notification Center for checking alerts.

7. **Control Center**: A gentle twist of the Digital Crown upwards from the watch face brings up the Control Center, allowing you to access settings like airplane mode, battery percentage, and more.

8. **Adjust Brightness and Volume**: In certain apps, like Music or during a call, the Digital Crown can adjust volume. Additionally, it can be used to adjust screen brightness.

9. **Time Travel**: When viewing the watch face, a twist of the Digital

Crown can show past and future events, weather forecasts, and more.

10. **Customizing Watch Faces**: While customizing a watch face, turning the Digital Crown can adjust various elements like complications, color schemes, and more.

The Digital Crown is a versatile tool that enhances the usability and functionality of the Apple Watch, providing an intuitive way to navigate and interact with the device. Its combination of rotational and pressing actions allows for a wide range of functions.

Apple Watch Series 9 comes equipped with a range of built-in apps designed to enhance various aspects of your daily life. From health and fitness to communication and productivity, these apps offer a seamless experience right on your wrist. Here are the most important apps you will find on the S9 watch:

**Sleep App**

This app helps you establish a healthy sleep routine by tracking your sleep patterns and providing personalized recommendations. Wear your Apple Watch to bed, and it will monitor your movements to determine your sleep quality and duration. You can open the Sleep app on your Apple Watch or set up sleep schedules via the Health app on your iPhone. The app is good for users looking to improve their sleep habits, monitor sleep trends, and optimize their rest.

**Noise App**

This app safeguards your hearing by alerting you when ambient noise reaches potentially harmful levels. It uses the watch's microphone to monitor surrounding sound levels and provides notifications if it detects excessive noise. The Noise app is accessible directly from the app grid on your Apple Watch.

**Cycle Tracking App**

Designed for individuals who menstruate, this app helps track menstrual cycles and provides valuable insights into fertility and reproductive health. Users input data about their menstrual cycle, including flow intensity and symptoms, and the app provides predictions and analysis. Find the Cycle Tracking app in the Health app on your paired iPhone. It will automatically be available on your Apple Watch.

**Messages App**

This app allows you to send and receive messages directly from your wrist, complete with voice dictation and emoji support. You can dictate messages, scribble, or use predefined responses. It also supports sending animated emojis and images. Rather than take out your iPhone, you can use the watch's message app for quick and convenient access to messaging.

## ECG (Electrocardiogram)

The ECG app on the Apple Watch Series allows users to take an electrocardiogram, providing insights into heart health. It measures the electrical activity of your heart over a period, generating a detailed report which can be shared with a healthcare provider. Individuals with heart health concerns or those monitoring their heart for any irregularities will find the ECG app useful.

## News

This app delivers curated news stories based on your preferences, ensuring you stay updated with the latest happenings. It offers a selection of articles from various news sources, allowing you to customize the topics and sources you're interested in.

## Mindfulness

The Mindfulness app encourages mental well-being through guided breathing exercises and moments of reflection. It offers short sessions to help calm the mind, reduce stress, and improve overall mental health. This app is ideal for persons looking for quick, accessible ways to practice mindfulness and improve mental clarity.

## Remote

This app transforms your Apple Watch into a remote control for various Apple devices, including Apple TV, iTunes, and more. It connects wirelessly to your devices, allowing you to control playback, adjust volume, and navigate menus. The Remote app is available in the watchOS system and can be found on your Apple Watch's app grid.

## Walkie-Talkie

Walkie-Talkie enables instant voice communication with other Apple Watch users who have the app enabled. Users send and receive voice messages in real-time, creating a quick and efficient means of communication.

## Phone App

This app allows you to make and receive calls directly from your Apple Watch, even if your iPhone is not nearby. It utilizes the watch's built-in speaker and microphone for phone calls, providing a convenient hands-free option.

Using App Store on the Series 9 Watch

The App Store on your Apple Watch
Series offers a curated selection of apps
designed to enhance your wearable
experience. Here's how you can
download and manage apps directly from
your wrist:

To download app;

- On your Apple Watch, locate and
  tap the App Store icon in the app
  grid.
- Browse through the available
  categories or use the search
  feature to find a specific app.
- Tap the app you want to
  download. You'll see an overview,
  along with an option to install. Tap
  "Install."

If prompted, authenticate the installation with your Apple ID, Face ID, or passcode. You'll see a progress indicator. Once the app is downloaded, it will automatically appear on your Apple Watch's app grid.

Here are some ways to manage apps on the S9 watch.

- **Reorganize the App Grid**: On the app grid, press and hold any app icon until it starts to wiggle. Then, drag it to a new position.

- **Deleting Apps**: While in edit mode (apps are wiggling), tap the 'X' icon on an app you want to delete. Confirm by tapping "Delete."

- **Offloading Apps**: Go to the Watch app on your paired iPhone. Navigate to "App Store" and toggle on "App Offloading." This allows the watch to automatically manage app storage.

- **Updating Apps**: Open the App Store on your Apple Watch. Navigate to the "Updates" tab at the bottom. If updates are available, tap "Update" next to each app or "Update All" at the top.

Using the Watch App on iPhone

- Open the Watch app on your iPhone.
- Navigate to "App Store" to browse and install apps on your Apple Watch.
- Under "My Watch," go to "General" and toggle on "Automatic App Install" to have

apps automatically installed on your watch when downloaded on your iPhone.

- In the Watch app on your iPhone, go to "General" > "Usage" to see how much space your apps are using. From there, you can offload or delete apps to free up storage.

- In the Watch app on your iPhone, go to "My Watch" and scroll down to view a list of installed apps. Toggle them on or off to control their presence on your watch.

How to Use Siri on Apple S9 Watch

Siri on your Apple Watch Series 9 allows you to perform tasks and get information using voice commands. It is easy to activate this unique Apple virtual assistant feature on your watch. Simply raise your wrist or press and hold the Digital Crown until you hear the Siri tone. You'll see a visual indication that Siri is listening. After the Siri tone, speak your command clearly and naturally. For example, "What's the weather today?" or "Set a timer for 10 minutes."

Siri will process your request and respond audibly with the information or perform the task. You can also read Siri's responses on the watch face if you prefer not to use audio.

**Useful Siri Commands**

Siri on your Apple Watch Series 9 can assist you with a wide range of tasks. Here are some common and useful commands:

"Send a message to [Contact Name]."

"What's the weather like today?"

"Set a timer for [specific time]."

"Remind me to [task] at [time]."

"Call [Contact Name]."

"Open [app name]."

"Play [song/album/playlist]."

"Navigate to [location]."

"Translate [phrase] to [language]."

"What's the latest news?"

"What's my next calendar event?"

"Show me my workout progress."

You can choose whether Siri responds with voice, text, or both:

- Open the Watch app on your paired iPhone.

- Go to "Siri" and select "Voice Feedback."
- Choose from options like "Always On," "Control with Silent Mode," or "Headphones Only."

**Type to Siri and Siri Pause Time**:

- Open the Settings app on your Apple Watch.
- Scroll down and tap "Accessibility."
- Tap "Siri" and enable "Type to Siri" if you prefer to type your commands.
- You can also adjust the "Siri Response" time.

Delete Siri History:

- On your iPhone, go to "Settings" > "Siri & Search."

- Tap "Siri & Dictation History."
- Select "Delete Siri & Dictation History" to clear your Siri history.

Note: Siri history is not stored on Apple servers, and deleting it only removes it from your device.

Setting Up Wallet and Apple Pay

Setting up Apple Pay on your Apple Watch allows for convenient and secure payments using your wrist-worn device. Here's how to do it:

- On your paired iPhone, open the Apple Watch app.
- Tap "Wallet & Apple Pay" from the list of available options.
- Tap "Add Card" and follow the on-screen instructions. You'll have the option to use a card already

associated with your Apple ID or manually enter a new card.

- If required, your bank will ask for verification through a one-time passcode or other method.
- Follow the prompts to set up Face ID or Touch ID for added security during transactions.

**Adding a Card to Apple Watch with iPhone**

- Open the Wallet app on your iPhone.
- Tap the "+" sign to add a new card.
- Enter the card details manually or use your iPhone's camera to capture them.
- Follow any additional verification steps provided by your bank.

If you are no longer using a card, remove it by opening the Wallet app on your Apple Watch. Tap on the card you want to remove. Finally, scroll down and tap "Remove This Card."

## Making Purchases with Apple Watch

- With Apple Pay activated, double-click the side button on your Apple Watch.
- Hold your Apple Watch close to the contactless payment reader until a check mark appears, indicating the payment is complete.

Passes in Wallet on Apple Watch S9

Passes in the Wallet app refer to digital cards or tickets, such as boarding passes, event tickets, coupons, and loyalty cards. They provide easy access to information and can be scanned or used at supported locations. To add a pass:

- Receive a digital pass via email or message. Tap the link to add it to your Wallet.
- Open the Wallet app on your Apple Watch.
- Select the pass you want to use.
- Hold your watch near the scanner or reader.

With Apple Pay and passes on your Apple Watch, you have a seamless and secure way to make purchases and access digital cards or tickets while on the go.

The Apple Watch S9 is an incredibly powerful tool for tracking and improving your fitness. It provides a wide range of features and apps to help you monitor your physical activity, set goals, and maintain a healthy lifestyle.

Tracking Fitness, Activities, and Achievements

The Workouts app on your Apple Watch allows you to choose from a variety of activities to track. To use this app:

- Tap the Workouts app icon on your Apple Watch.
- Scroll through the list of available activities (e.g., running, cycling,

swimming, yoga) and choose the one you're about to do.

- Customize your workout by setting a specific goal like time, distance, or calories burned.
- Tap "Start" to begin tracking. You can pause and resume the workout as needed.
- During your workout, swipe left to see real-time metrics like heart rate, pace, distance, and more.

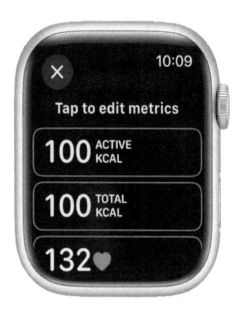

- When you're finished, swipe right and tap "End" to save the workout.
- On your paired iPhone, open the Fitness app to see detailed records of your workouts.

The Activity app helps you keep track of your daily movements and sets personalized goals. It consists of three rings:

- Move Ring (Red): Tracks the calories you've burned throughout the day based on your movement.
- Exercise Ring (Green): Measures the time spent doing brisk activity that gets your heart rate up.
- Stand Ring (Blue): Monitors how often you stand up and move around for at least one minute each hour.

Achievements are virtual awards you earn for hitting milestones or accomplishing fitness goals. They serve as motivational markers of your progress. Some examples include reaching your Move goal every day for a week or completing a certain number of workouts in a month.

The "Move" target on Apple Watch is a customizable goal for the number of active calories you aim to burn in a day. It's important to set a Move goal that aligns with your personal fitness level, activity level, and overall health objectives. Here are some general guidelines to help you determine a good Move target:

1. Consider your current fitness level. If you're just starting out, a lower Move goal can be a good

initial target. As you progress, you can gradually increase it.

2. If you have specific health goals or concerns, it's advisable to consult with a healthcare professional or a fitness expert. They can provide personalized advice on setting a Move goal that's appropriate for you.

3. It's often recommended to set a Move goal that challenges you but is still achievable. Gradually increase it over time as your fitness improves.

4. Instead of focusing solely on daily goals, consider your average active calories burned over a week. This can provide a more balanced perspective on your overall activity levels.

5.  Pay attention to how your body
    feels during and after workouts. If
    you consistently feel fatigued or
    overworked, it may be an
    indication that your Move goal is
    set too high.

6.  Remember to factor in rest days or
    lighter activity days when setting
    your Move goal. It's important to
    allow your body time to recover.

7.  Be flexible with your Move goal. If
    your daily routine or activity levels
    change (e.g., due to work or
    travel), consider adjusting your
    goal accordingly.

8.  Use the Activity app to track your
    progress and see how
    consistently you meet your Move
    goal. This can help you make
    informed adjustments.

Advanced Health Features

The Apple Watch Series 9 comes with features to help you monitor your heart rate or oxygen levels. The heart rate measurement is taken by the optical sensors on the back of the Apple Watch, which monitor the blood flow through your wrist. The heart rate app provides real-time reading. For continuous monitoring during workouts, you can use the Workout app or enable "Continuous Heart Rate" in the Health app on your iPhone. You can also view your heart rate during a workout by swiping left on the workout screen. To get the most accurate readings, ensure that the back of the Apple Watch is in direct contact with your skin, and the band is snug but not too tight. To check your heart rate on an Apple Watch, follow these steps:

- If you're on the watch face, press
  the Digital Crown to go to the app
  grid. Look for the "Heart Rate" app
  icon, which looks like a heart.
- Tap on the "Heart Rate" app to
  open it.

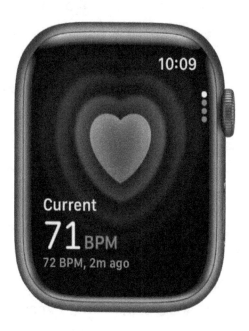

- Your Apple Watch will take a few
  moments to measure your heart

rate. Ensure the watch is snug on your wrist for accurate readings.

- Once the measurement is complete, your current heart rate will be displayed on the screen.

To measure your blood oxygen levels on an Apple Watch, follow these steps:

- Raise your wrist or tap the display to wake up your Apple Watch.
- If you're on the watch face, press the Digital Crown to go to the app grid. Look for the "Blood Oxygen" app icon, which looks like a red and blue gradient circle.
- Tap on the "Blood Oxygen" app to open it.
- Follow the on-screen instructions, which typically involve keeping

your arm still and flat while the watch takes a measurement.

- Your Apple Watch will take a few moments to measure your blood oxygen levels.
- Once the measurement is complete, your current blood oxygen level will be displayed on the screen.

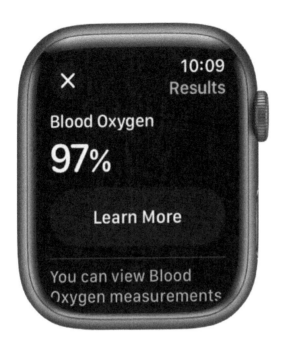

The blood oxygen measurement is taken by the optical sensors on the back of the Apple Watch, which use infrared light to measure the color of your blood. Blood oxygen measurements can be affected by factors like altitude, physical activity, skin tone, and the fit of the watch.

Remember, while the Apple Watch provides a convenient way to monitor your heart rate, it is not a replacement for professional medical advice or diagnosis. If you have any concerns about your heart health, consult a healthcare provider.Raise your wrist or tap the display to wake up your Apple Watch.

Sleep Tracking and Improving Sleep Habits

With the Sleep app on your S9 watch, you have the ability to establish sleep schedules that align with your sleep objectives. By wearing your watch while you sleep, your Apple Watch diligently monitors your rest, estimating the time spent in different sleep stages, including REM, Core, and Deep, and even providing insights into potential wake-up moments.

Upon waking, a quick visit to the Sleep app reveals the duration of your sleep and offers a comprehensive view of your sleep patterns over the past two weeks. Should your Apple Watch's battery fall below 30 percent prior to bedtime, you'll receive a timely reminder to charge it. In the morning, a quick glance at the screen will show you the remaining battery life.

The Sleep app on your Apple Watch monitors your sleep patterns and provides insights into your sleep quality. Here's how to use it:

**Set Up Sleep Schedule**

Open the Health app on your paired iPhone. Tap "Browse" > "Sleep" > "Get

Started." Set your desired sleep schedule and goals.

**Wear Your Apple Watch to Bed**

Ensure your watch is charged enough to last through the night. Enable "Sleep Mode" to reduce screen brightness and prevent disturbances.

**View Sleep Data**

In the Sleep app, you can view your sleep duration, time in bed, and trends over time.

Ways to Integrate Your Apple Watch with
Gym Equipment

Integrating your Apple Watch with fitness
equipment can enhance your workout
experience by providing more accurate
data and seamless tracking. Here are
several ways to do it:

**GymKit Integration**

GymKit is a feature that allows your Apple Watch to communicate with compatible gym equipment, sharing information like heart rate, distance, and more for a more accurate workout tracking. Simply tap your Apple Watch on a GymKit-enabled machine, and it will automatically sync with your watch.

**Pairing with Treadmills and Bikes**

Many modern treadmills and stationary bikes have Bluetooth or NFC capabilities that allow you to pair them with your Apple Watch. Once paired, your Apple Watch can provide real-time data on your workout, including heart rate, distance, and calories burned.

## Use Fitness Apps with WatchOS

Many popular fitness apps (e.g., Strava, Nike Training Club) are compatible with WatchOS and can sync seamlessly with your Apple Watch. You can start and track workouts directly from your watch, and the data is synced with the app on your iPhone.

Apple places a strong emphasis on accessibility, aiming to make their products inclusive for users with various disabilities. The Apple Watch Series 9 includes a range of features designed to enhance accessibility and usability for individuals with different needs. Here are some of the notable accessibility features:

How to Setup S9 Using VoiceOver

VoiceOver is a screen reader that provides spoken descriptions of what's happening on your Apple Watch, enabling users with visual impairments to navigate and interact with the device. It allows users to hear and interact with the interface, ensuring they can access all features and functions. Here are steps to set up an Apple Watch S9 using VoiceOver:

- Press and hold the side button until you hear the startup sound and feel a tap on your wrist.
- Swipe up or down on the screen to select your preferred language. Double-tap the screen to confirm.
- Bring your iPhone near the Apple Watch. A setup prompt will appear on your iPhone.
- Follow the instructions on your iPhone screen to pair the devices. This may involve using the iPhone's camera to scan an animation displayed on the Apple Watch.

- Once paired, you'll be asked to choose a wrist for wearing your Apple Watch.

- Next, you'll be prompted to set up VoiceOver. Swipe up or down to select "Set Up VoiceOver," then double-tap to confirm.

- Follow the on-screen instructions to set up other accessibility features, like Zoom, Larger Text, and Bold Text, if needed.

- If prompted, sign in with your Apple ID and complete the setup process on your iPhone.

- If you have a previous backup of your Apple Watch, you can choose to restore it at this stage.

How to Enable Zoom

Zoom magnifies the contents of the Apple Watch display, making it easier for users with low vision to read text and view details. It provides visual amplification, allowing users to see content more clearly.

Here's how you can use Zoom:

- From your Apple Watch home screen, press the Digital Crown to access the app grid.
- Find and tap on the "Settings" app, which is represented by a gear icon.
- Scroll down and tap on "Accessibility."
- In the Accessibility settings, locate and tap on "Zoom."

- Toggle the switch next to "Zoom" to enable the feature. You will see a zoomed-in version of the screen.
  - Zoom In: Double-tap the screen with two fingers to zoom in. This will increase the magnification level.
  - Pan Around: Drag two fingers around the screen to pan and explore different areas.
  - Zoom Out: Double-tap the screen with two fingers again to zoom out. Repeat as needed to adjust the level of magnification.
- Within the Zoom settings, you can customize options like Zoom Region (Fullscreen or Windowed), Zoom Filter (None, Inverted,

Greyscale, etc.), and Maximum
Zoom Level.

- To exit Zoom mode, double-tap
  the screen with two fingers and
  then tap "Zoom Out."
  Alternatively, you can press the
  Digital Crown to return to the
  home screen.

The Zoom feature is especially useful for
individuals with visual impairments or
those who may benefit from enhanced
screen magnification. Remember that
you can adjust the settings to suit your
preferences and needs.

How to Increase or Bold Text

This feature allows users to adjust the
text size across various apps, making it
easier to read for those with visual
impairments or difficulties. It enhances

readability, ensuring text is comfortably legible for users. You can adjust text size and other visual settings on your Apple Watch Series 9 using the steps below:

- From your Apple Watch home screen, press the Digital Crown to access the app grid.
- Find and tap on the "Settings" app, which is represented by a gear icon.
- Scroll down and tap on "Accessibility."
- Tap on "Display & Text Size."
- Use the slider under "Text Size" to increase or decrease the size of the text.
- Toggle the switch next to "Bold Text" to turn this feature on. This will make the text bolder and more prominent.

- Under "Display & Text Size," you'll find options to increase contrast:
  - Reduce Transparency: Toggling this switch can make elements on the screen more distinct by reducing the transparency effect.
  - On/Off Labels: Enabling this will add labels to toggle buttons, making it easier to distinguish their states.

How to Adjust Animations and Effects

This feature reduces the motion effects and animations on the Apple Watch, which can be helpful for users who may experience discomfort or motion sensitivity. It creates a more static interface, reducing potential motion-related discomfort. You can adjust motor skills settings and use Touch Accommodations features on your Apple Watch through the Accessibility options. Here's how you can do it:

- From your Apple Watch home screen, press the Digital Crown to access the app grid.
- Find and tap on the "Settings" app, which is represented by a gear icon.
- Scroll down and tap on "Accessibility."
- Tap on "Touch" to access touch-related settings.
- Toggle the switch next to "Touch Accommodations" to enable the feature.

- Once enabled, you can customize various touch-related settings to suit your needs:
  - Hold Duration: Adjust the length of time a touch must be held to register as a tap.
  - Ignore Repeat: Prevents rapid, repeated taps from registering.
  - Touch Accommodations Options: Explore various options like "Ignore Repeat," "Hold Duration," and "Hold Before Repeat" to fine-tune touch interactions.

How to Use Haptic Feedback

Apple Watch provides haptic feedback through vibrations, which can be particularly useful for users with hearing impairments or in situations where sound cues may not be sufficient. It ensures users receive important notifications and alerts through physical feedback. You can tell time on your Apple Watch using haptic feedback, which provides tactile sensations on your wrist to indicate the time. Here's how to do it:

- Raise your wrist or tap the display to wake up your Apple Watch.
- Press two fingers on the watch face and hold them there for a moment. You'll feel a series of taps in response.
- The haptic feedback will provide a series of short and long taps that correspond to the time.
  - Hours: A series of short taps indicate the hour. For

example, three short taps indicate 3 o'clock.

○ Minutes: A series of long taps indicate the minutes. For example, two long taps followed by three short taps indicate 23 minutes past the hour (or 3:23).

For instance, if you feel three short taps followed by two long taps and three short taps, it's indicating 3:23. Once you've determined the time, simply raise your wrist to return to the clock face.

How to Enable AssistiveTouch

This feature allows users to navigate and control the Apple Watch using gestures and on-screen buttons, which can be particularly helpful for users with mobility impairments. It provides an alternative interaction method for users who may have difficulty with touch gestures. Here's how to set up AssistiveTouch

- From your Apple Watch home screen, press the Digital Crown to access the app grid.
- Find and tap on the "Settings" app, which is represented by a gear icon.
- Scroll down and tap on "Accessibility."
- Tap on "Touch" to access touch-related settings.
- Toggle the switch next to "AssistiveTouch" to enable the feature.
- Tap on "AssistiveTouch" to customize the menu options.

- You can add or remove specific functions from the menu according to your needs.
- A small, circular icon will now appear on the screen. This is the AssistiveTouch menu. Tap the icon to open the menu, which provides various options for navigation and interaction.
  - Single Tap: Performs a standard tap.
  - Double Tap: Activates a predefined action (you can customize this in settings).
  - Long Press: Opens a menu with additional options.
  - Swipe: Allows for gestures like swipe up, swipe down, etc.

Once you've customized the settings and familiarized yourself with AssistiveTouch, you can press the Digital Crown to return to the home screen.

How to Setup Shortcuts on the S9 Watch

Apple Watch Series 9 offers powerful automation and shortcut features to streamline your daily tasks and routines. These tools can save you time and effort. Here's how to use them effectively:

- Open the Shortcuts app on your iPhone.
- Tap "Automation" at the bottom.
- Tap the "+" icon to create a new automation.
- Choose a trigger for your automation (e.g., time of day, location, app, etc.).

- Configure the specific actions you want to automate (e.g., sending a message, adjusting settings, etc.).
- Save and activate your automation.

Once you've created automations and shortcuts on your iPhone, they will automatically sync to your Apple Watch. On your Apple Watch, you can activate automations using the Shortcuts app or by adding a shortcut to the Siri watch face. Open the Shortcuts app on your watch and tap on the automation or shortcut to run it.

By leveraging automations and major shortcuts on your Apple Watch Series, you can simplify and expedite various tasks in your daily routine. Experiment with different triggers and actions to create personalized workflows that suit your needs. Remember to regularly review and refine your automations and shortcuts for optimal efficiency.

Apple Watch Series 9 seamlessly integrates with various Apple devices, enhancing your overall experience. You can connect several devices to perform different actions with ease. By integrating with other Apple devices, the Apple Watch Series 9 enhances convenience, productivity, and connectivity in your everyday life. This ecosystem of devices ensures a seamless and unified user experience.

## Setting Up Continuity Features

Continuity features are a set of functionalities introduced by Apple to create a seamless and integrated experience across various Apple devices. These features allow for smooth transitions between devices and enhance the overall user experience. Here are some key continuity features:

- **Handoff**: Handoff allows you to start an activity on one Apple device and continue it on another. For example, you can begin composing an email on your iPhone and seamlessly switch to your Mac to finish it.

- **Universal Clipboard**: This feature enables you to copy text, images, or files on one Apple device and paste them on another. It simplifies the process of moving content between devices.

- **Auto Unlock**: When wearing an authenticated Apple Watch S9, you can automatically unlock your

Mac without entering a password when you're in close proximity.

- **Instant Hotspot**: If you're out of Wi-Fi range but have a cellular-enabled iPhone nearby, you can use it as a personal hotspot without manually configuring settings.

- **AirDrop**: AirDrop allows you to wirelessly share files, photos, and other content between Apple devices with just a few taps.

- **Apple Pay**: You can use Apple Pay on your Mac or iPad to make online purchases securely without having to enter credit card details.

- **Continuity Camera**: This feature lets you use your iPhone's camera to take photos or scan documents directly into applications on your Mac.

- **Handoff for Safari**: You can open a web page on one device and continue browsing it on another by clicking the Handoff icon in the dock.

- **Live Photos and Continuity**: You can view Live Photos on your Mac or iPad, and they play as a short video clip when you hover over them.

- **Notes and Continuity**: You can start a note on one device and pick up where you left off on another.

- **Documents in the Cloud**: This allows you to work on the same document across multiple Apple devices, with changes automatically synchronized.

Ways to Use Apple Watch Series 9 and iPhone Together

Remember, the strength of the Apple Watch-iPhone pairing lies in their seamless integration. This allows for a cohesive user experience across both devices, enhancing convenience and productivity. The Apple Watch and iPhone work seamlessly together, offering a range of functionalities. Here are ways you can use them together:

**Fitness Tracking and Health Monitoring**

The Apple Watch is a powerful fitness tracker. It can monitor your heart rate, track your workouts, count steps, and even remind you to stand and move throughout the day. All this data syncs with the Health app on your iPhone for a comprehensive overview of your health and fitness.

**Receive Notifications and Alerts**

The Apple Watch allows you to receive notifications for calls, messages, emails, and apps directly on your wrist. This keeps you updated without needing to take out your phone.

**Make and Answer Calls**

With the Apple Watch, you can make and answer phone calls directly from your wrist. It serves as a convenient hands-free option when your phone isn't readily accessible.

**Send and Receive Messages**

You can send and receive messages on your Apple Watch using Siri, quick replies, or even by drawing out individual letters.

**Apple Pay and Wallet**

Use your Apple Watch for contactless payments with Apple Pay. It's a secure and convenient way to make transactions without pulling out your iPhone.

**Navigation and Maps**

The Apple Watch provides turn-by-turn directions right on your wrist. It also offers haptic feedback, making it easy to navigate without needing to constantly check your iPhone.

**Remote Control for iPhone Camera**

The Apple Watch can serve as a remote control for your iPhone's camera. This is particularly useful for group photos or capturing shots from a distance.

## Music and Podcast Control

Control playback of music and podcasts on your iPhone using your Apple Watch. You can adjust volume, skip tracks, and play or pause with ease.

## Voice Assistant Integration with Siri

Both the Apple Watch and iPhone have Siri, Apple's voice-activated assistant. You can use Siri on your watch to set reminders, send messages, get directions, and perform various other tasks.

Using Apple Watch S9 for Smart Homes

Controlling your smart home with an Apple Watch Series 9 is a convenient way to manage your devices without having to reach for your phone. Before setting up, make sure your smart home devices are compatible with Apple's HomeKit platform. Most popular smart home brands support HomeKit, but it's always good to double-check. Here's a step-by-step guide on how to set up and use your Apple Watch for smart home control:

- Open the "Home" app on your iPhone.
- Tap the "+" icon to add a new accessory or scene.
- Follow the on-screen instructions to add your smart home devices to

HomeKit. Make sure they are connected to your Wi-Fi network.

- Arrange your devices into rooms and assign them to specific scenes for easy control. For example, group your lights into the "Living Room" or "Bedroom" category.

- Next, you have to sync HomeKit with iCloud by opening the "Settings" app on your iPhone. Tap your Apple ID at the top. Select "iCloud" and ensure that "Home" is enabled. This allows your HomeKit data to sync with your Apple Watch.

- **Install the Home App on Your Apple Watch**. Open the "Watch" app on your iPhone. Scroll down to "Available Apps" and find "Home." Tap "Install" next to it.

- **Access the Home App on Your Apple Watch**. Press the Digital Crown on your Apple Watch to go to the home screen. Find and tap the "Home" app icon. It looks like a house.

- **Control Your Smart Devices**: In the Home app on your Apple Watch, you'll see a list of rooms and scenes you've set up. Tap a room to see the devices within it. Tap a device to toggle it on or off, adjust settings, or activate specific scenes.

- **Use Siri for Voice Control**: You can also use Siri on your Apple Watch to control your smart home. Just raise your wrist and say, "Hey

Siri," followed by your command. For example, "Hey Siri, turn off the lights in the living room."

- **Create Automation and Scenes**: Open the Home app on your iPhone. Tap "Automation" at the bottom. Create automation based on time, location, sensor input, or the state of other accessories. For example, you can set up a "Good Morning" scene that turns on the lights and adjusts the thermostat when you wake up.

The Apple Watch comes equipped with various safety features designed to enhance the well-being and security of its users. For instance, there is the fall detection feature. When a significant fall is detected, the watch will prompt the user to confirm if they are okay. If no response is received, the watch can automatically contact emergency services and share your location with them.

Also, you can have access to the Emergency SOS feature. Thanks to this feature, you can quickly contact local emergency services by pressing and holding the side button on the Apple Watch. It will then dial the emergency number for your region and share your location.

The Apple Watch can monitor your heart rate and notify you if it detects an irregular rhythm that may be a sign of atrial fibrillation (AFib). The watch can send an alert if it detects that your heart rate rises to a level that is unusually high when you're inactive. This can be an indicator of potential health issues.

Before swimming, you can activate the Water Lock feature to prevent accidental taps and touches on the screen. After swimming, you can use the "Eject Water" feature to expel water from the speaker. Remember, while these features can enhance safety and provide peace of mind, they are not a substitute for professional medical advice or emergency services. Always seek appropriate help in the case of a genuine emergency or medical concern.

Setting Up Medical ID

Setting up and viewing your Medical ID on an Apple Watch is a straightforward process. The Medical ID feature allows you to store critical health information that can be accessed in case of an emergency. Remember to keep your Medical ID up to date, especially if there are any changes in your health status or emergency contacts. This ensures that the information is accurate and useful in case of an emergency. Here's how you can do it:

- Open the "Health" app on your iPhone. It typically has a white icon with a red heart.

- In the bottom-right corner, tap on the "Profile" icon.
- Tap on "Medical ID."

- Click on "Edit" at the top right corner.
- Enter important information such as your name, date of birth, medical conditions, allergies, medications, and emergency contacts. Be as detailed as possible.

- Make sure the toggle switch for "Show When Locked" is turned on. This allows anyone to access your Medical ID from the lock screen.

- You can add emergency contacts by tapping "add emergency contact." These contacts will also be accessible from the lock screen when someone tries to access your Medical ID.

- Once you've entered all necessary information, tap "Done" to save your changes.

- To view Medical ID on Apple Watch, press and hold the side button (just below the Digital Crown) on your Apple Watch.

- When the Power Off screen appears, swipe right on the

"Emergency SOS" slider. This will take you to your Medical ID.

How to Contact Emergency Services

To contact emergency services using your Apple Watch, you can use the Emergency SOS feature. Follow these steps:

- Press and hold the side button on your Apple Watch (located just below the Digital Crown) until the Emergency SOS slider appears.

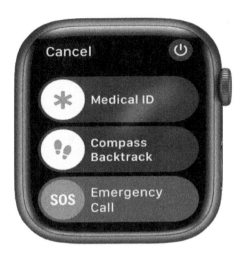

- Drag the Emergency SOS slider to the right. This will start a countdown timer.

- Continue holding the slider until the countdown timer finishes. This is typically set to 3 seconds.

- Once the countdown is complete, your Apple Watch will automatically dial the local emergency services number based on your location.

- When the call connects, you'll be in contact with an emergency operator. Be sure to clearly explain the situation and provide any necessary details.

If you have a cellular-enabled Apple Watch, it can make the call even if your iPhone is not nearby or turned on, as long as it is connected to a cellular network. If you have a GPS-enabled Apple Watch and it's connected to your iPhone, it will also send your location to the emergency services.

How to Set Up Fall Detection

Fall Detection is designed to detect significant falls and offer immediate assistance in case of emergencies. It uses a custom algorithm to analyze your wrist trajectory and impact acceleration.

If it detects a fall, it will initiate a response. Upon detecting a significant fall, the watch will tap you on the wrist, sound an alarm, and display an alert. You have the option to dismiss the alert if you're okay. If the watch senses that you're immobile or unresponsive after the fall, it will automatically initiate an emergency call. It also sends a message with your location to your emergency contacts.

You can adjust the sensitivity of the fall detection feature in the Apple Watch settings. This allows you to fine-tune it based on your activity level and personal needs.

Fall Detection can be particularly beneficial for older adults, individuals with mobility issues, or those at a higher risk of accidents. In case of a significant fall, the watch can automatically call for help if you're unable to do so yourself. This can be a critical feature for individuals at risk of falls, such as seniors.

Setting Up Fall Detection:

- Open the "Apple Watch" app on your paired iPhone.

- Tap "My Watch" at the bottom, then scroll down and select "Emergency SOS."

- Toggle on the switch next to "Fall Detection." You may be prompted to confirm this action.

- Below sensitivity settings, you can add emergency contacts. These will be notified in case a fall is detected.

- If you want to verify that Fall Detection is working correctly, you can perform a controlled fall (with care) and observe if the alert is triggered.

Remember, Fall Detection is not foolproof, and it may not detect all falls. It's an additional layer of safety but does not replace professional medical assistance if needed. Always seek appropriate help in case of a genuine emergency or medical concern.

Troubleshooting Common Issues

In the course of utilizing any technology, occasional hiccups are inevitable. The "Apple Watch Series 9 Guide" stands as a reliable companion not only in moments of discovery but also in times of need. It offers astute advice and systematic troubleshooting for some of the most frequently encountered issues:

**Battery Drain and Performance Optimization**:

One of the recurring concerns with any wearable device is battery life. The guide furnishes readers with a comprehensive set of strategies to maximize battery efficiency. It offers insights into managing

120

background processes, optimizing settings, and identifying power-hungry apps.

**Syncing and Connectivity Challenges**:

Seamless synchronization with your iPhone is fundamental to the Apple Watch experience. The eBook presents a range of solutions for troubleshooting connectivity issues, including resetting network settings and ensuring proper Bluetooth connections.

**Software Updates and Installation Problems**:

Staying up-to-date with the latest software is paramount for optimal performance. This guide offers a systematic approach to tackling any hiccups encountered during the update process, ensuring that users can leverage the newest features and security enhancements.

**Health and Fitness Data Accuracy**:

For users who rely heavily on the Apple Watch for health tracking, accuracy is of utmost importance. The eBook delves into potential issues with sensor readings and provides guidance on recalibration and ensuring accurate health data.

**App Crashes and Unresponsive Behavior**:

The occasional app crash or unresponsive behavior can be frustrating. The guide introduces readers to methods for force-quitting apps, clearing caches, and ensuring smooth operation.

**Customization and Personalization Challenges**:

Tailoring the Apple Watch to individual preferences is a key aspect of its appeal. In the face of any challenges in this domain, the eBook offers detailed solutions, ensuring users can craft an experience uniquely their own.

## Conclusion

In the digital landscape of wearable technology, this guide emerges as an invaluable companion for both new adopters and seasoned users of Apple S9 watches. As we conclude this exploration of its contents, it is evident that this eBook encapsulates the epitome of expertise and user-friendliness. Its comprehensive coverage ranges from initial setup to intricate features, leaving no stone unturned in unraveling the full potential of the Apple Watch Series 9.

For the uninitiated, this guide serves as an illuminating beacon, ushering them into the world of wearable technology. Its detailed explanations and step-by-step instructions transform the learning curve into an enjoyable and empowering journey. From configuring personalized watch faces to harnessing the potential of advanced health monitoring, every facet of the Apple Watch experience is demystified.

Yet, the brilliance of this guide is not confined to novices alone. Seasoned users will find themselves delving into hitherto unexplored territories, discovering hidden gems within the Series 9's array of features. The eBook's adept coverage of the latest enhancements ensures that even long-standing Apple Watch enthusiasts can glean fresh insights and optimize their experience to unprecedented levels.

This guide is a gateway to a world of boundless possibilities, equipping users with the knowledge and skills to extract the utmost from their Apple Watch. Its troubleshooting section, in particular, serves as a guardian against common pitfalls, ensuring a seamless and uninterrupted experience for every user. As technology continues to evolve, this guide stands as an enduring companion, ready to empower both new and seasoned users in their journey with the Apple Watch Series 9.

Printed in the USA
CPSIA information can be obtained
at www.ICGtesting.com
LVHW011615260624
784066LV00010B/518

9 798869 756862